25 KEYS
TO A HAPPY LIFE

From the Qu'ran and Sunnah

ISMAIL KAMDAR

25 Keys to a Happy Life

First Published in England by
Kube Publishing Ltd
MCC, Ratby Lane, Markfield
Leicestershire, LE67 9SY
United Kingdom
Tel: +44 (0) 1530 249230
Website: www.kubepublishing.com
Email: info@kubepublishing.com

Cataloguing-in-Publication Data is available from the British Library.

ISBN 978-1-84774-237-7 Hardback
ISBN 978-1-84774-238-4 Ebook

Editor: Malika Kahn
Cover Design and typesetting: Afreen Fazil (Jaryah Studios)
*Printed in:*Turkey by Elma Basim

CONTENTS

CHASING HAPPINESS

IN THE NAME OF ALLAH,
MOST GRACIOUS, MOST MERCIFUL

All praise is for Allah, the Merciful, the Loving. Peace be upon His final Messenger, the mercy to this universe, Muhammad ﷺ, and all those who follow his way with righteousness until the end of time.

Happiness is something every human seeks. We all want to be happy. Nobody wakes up in the morning hoping to have a sad day or purposely seeks out a way to make themselves miserable. Yet too often, the paths we choose in search of happiness actually take us away from it, deeper into despair and misguidance.

The modern world is obsessed with the pursuit of happiness. Entire cultures are developed around chasing happiness, which seems ever elusive. It seems like no matter how free a person gets, how wealthy or famous they become, or how many possessions they pile up, happiness is still outside their grasp. It does not help that their definition of happiness is vague and subjective.

What if happiness does not lie in what they chase? What if the path of happiness is often the opposite of modernity? What is happiness, and how do we achieve it? This book seeks to answer this question through reflections from the Qur'an and Sunnah.

As Muslims, we believe that Allah created us to worship Him. This is our purpose, and any life that is lacking in its purpose will never experience true happiness. Allah's revelation, which reaches us through the Qur'an (the Word of Allah) and the Sunnah (the practical teachings of his Last Prophet ﷺ), gives us guidance on every aspect of life, including how to achieve true happiness.

In this book, we will discover what makes a human soul truly happy. It is not possessions, fame, or desires. True happiness is gained from living a life that is pleasing to God, finding inner peace and contentment, refining our skills, character, and manners; and building strong relationships with good people. Happiness is not selfish or self-centred. It is the result of living a life that is natural and purposeful. Let us now explore the keys to a truly happy life.

Ismail Kamdar

27 Ramadan 1444

LIVE A LIFE
OF PURPOSE

وَمَا خَلَقْنَا السَّمَاوَاتِ وَالْأَرْضَ وَمَا بَيْنَهُمَا لَاعِبِينَ

*Wa maa khalaqnas samaawaati wal arda
wa maa baina humaa laa'ibeen*

**And We did not create the heavens and
the earth and that between them in vain**
(Surah al-Dukhan 44:38)

People often look for happiness in mindless consump-
tion and entertainment. Wrongly assuming that happiness can be found in entertaining oneself to death,
they soon discover the opposite. A life of mindless fun
without any greater purpose is an empty experience
that is depressing and frustrating.

Over the years, I have met many converts whose stor-
ies started like this. They were focused on entertaining themselves and indulging their desires, only
to discover that it did not bring any happiness to their
lives. They only become truly happy after embracing
Islam and shifting their focus to living a purposeful
life. When life is focused on its one true purpose, it

becomes meaningful, and this leads to inner peace and happiness.

Islam is the only religion that clearly defines the purpose of life. We know that Allah created us to worship Him. He created this universe as a place to test us. Allah gave us free will so that we can pass or fail the test through our own choices and actions. He sent prophets and revealed scriptures so that the truth is clear for anyone who seeks it. It is through this scripture that we learn the purpose of our lives; to worship Allah.

وَمَا خَلَقْتُ الْجِنَّ وَالْإِنْسَ إِلَّا لِيَعْبُدُونِ

Wa maa khalaqtul jinna wal insa illaa liya'budoon

**I did not create jinn nor humans except
to worship Me (Surah al-Dhariyat 51:56)**

Worship in Islam does not mean focusing all one's time on ritual acts of worship. It has a much broader meaning. There are specific rituals that we need to do like praying five times a day and fasting the month of Ramadan. These are necessary and a priority. Beyond that, worship can be done simply by living a life that is pleasing to Allah.

Anytime we consciously choose to obey Allah, we are worshipping Him. Whether it is by earning halal, taking care of our families, or helping our communities, it is all worship when it is done for Allah. Our purpose, then, is to live a life that is pleasing to the Creator. This is what is missing in many people's lives

They pursue happiness through desires, wealth, entertainment, and personal relationships, but something always feels like it is missing. A life that is pleasing to the Creator is the only thing that can fill this void.

Because the definition of worship is so broad, every Muslim can choose different careers and paths in life and still live a life that is pleasing to Allah. If we fulfil our basic obligations and keep things halal, any career can become a life of purpose. So, the counsellor who offers therapy to benefit God's creation, and the doctor who serves their community through saving lives, and the scholar who teaches the religion, are all worshipping Allah in different ways.

Find a path for yourself that is pleasing to Allah and beneficial to others. Once you find something you are skilled at, develop yourself until you become a leader in that field. Eventually, you will find yourself living a purposeful life that provides halal income, benefits society, and is pleasing to Allah. When life is purposeful, we experience true happiness and inner peace.

BUILD YOUR AFTERLIFE

The Messenger ﷺ said, "When the person dies, their deeds end except for three: ongoing charity, beneficial knowledge, or a righteous child who prays for them."

(Sahih Muslim 1631)

Do not be afraid of death. For the believer, death is not the end. It is simply the end of the test, and hopefully the beginning of eternal bliss. True happiness can only be experienced after death, when the trials of life are over, and we enter the eternal garden. This is the happiness that every Muslim strives for.

Our lives are short, and we do not know how long we have left in this world. We want our deeds to outlive us so that they continue to pile up long after we have passed away. To accomplish this, we must focus a portion of our lives on building sources of continuous reward. Any good deed that continues to benefit people after you pass away can be a source of continuous reward if your intention is pure.

In general, there are three broad categories of such deeds: charity, knowledge, and descendants. Any charity we give that has long-term effects on society will continue to be a source of reward for us for as long as people benefit from it. For example, if you build a well in a community that needs one, even if people are still drinking from that well a hundred years later, you will still be rewarded for each person who benefits from it.

Likewise, if we donate to orphanages, build homes for those devastated by natural disasters, build masjids, sponsor orphans, or establish centres to protect victims of abuse, each of these becomes a source of continuous reward for the one who contributed to it. Therefore, we must invest our extra income in sources of continuous reward to ensure that our wealth continues to benefit us in the Afterlife, long after we have left this world.

The same applies to knowledge. If you teach someone anything beneficial, you are rewarded for as long as they benefit from that knowledge. Just as we focus on investing our wealth in sources of continuous charity, we must do the same for our knowledge. We can do this by developing educational media, establishing schools, universities, and libraries, writing books, teaching local children, and sponsoring the university fees of others. The more you invest in the education of others, the more sources of continuous reward you establish.

The third category of continuous reward is descendants who pray for us. Imagine if a hundred years after you have passed away, your grandchildren and great-grandchildren are still mentioning you by name and praying for you. Having children and raising them in a way that is pleasing to Allah is one of the best ways to invest in the Afterlife. If they grow up to be righteous, then they and their descendants also become sources of continuous reward for you.

Death is inescapable, but we can prepare for it by dedicating a portion of our wealth and knowledge to benefiting others, and by raising the next generation to worship Allah. When we do this, death is no longer a depressing or scary reality. The believer meets Allah with hope in His Reward, excited about the happiness that lies on the other side.

DO NOT OPEN THE DOOR OF "IF ONLY"

The Messenger ﷺ said, "Strive for that which will benefit you, seek the help of Allah, and do not feel helpless. If anything befalls you, do not say, 'If only I had done such and such' rather say 'Allah has decreed and whatever He wills, He does' because 'if' opens (the door) to the deeds of Satan."

(Ibn Majah 79)

t is tempting to look back at our past mistakes and think "if only I did this differently, my life would be better now". But these thoughts are unproductive and distract us from what is within our control. It is part of the devil's plan to distract us and depress us with obsession over the past. He wants us to become so bogged down with regrets that we do not see the blessings in front of us or the way forward. All we see are the regrets of the past.

But the past is the past, and there is nothing anyone can do to change it. The only way forward is to focus on building a better future. There is no point obsessing over what has already passed. That was your destiny and it was meant to happen. Instead, learn from it, grow from it, and focus on the present and the future. The lessons from our past should propel us to do better and inspire us to be better in our future.

The past cannot be altered, but we can build upon it. Do not obsess over "if only". Instead, focus on "what next". Because the future has not been revealed to you, approach it with optimism, excitement, and firm trust in Allah's Plan. Do this, and you will find yourself more excited about life. An optimistic view of the future is far better than a depressing obsession with the past.

"Know that what has passed you by [and you have failed to attain] was not going to befall you, and what has befallen you was not going to pass you by."

(Nawawi's 40 Hadith 19)

THINK GOOD THOUGHTS ABOUT ALLAH

The Messenger ﷺ said, "Allah says: 'I am as My slave thinks of Me, and I am with him if He remembers Me.'"

(Sahih al-Bukhari 7405)

What do you think about your Creator? Do you view Him as a vengeful, angry god waiting to punish you for your sins? Or do you view Him as a Merciful, Loving God looking for reasons to forgive you and accept you into Paradise? The way you view your Creator affects how you live your life and your overall happiness.

In some cultures, there is too much focus on Allah's wrath during the early years of education. Because of this, children develop an unhealthy fear of Allah that is not rooted in the love of Allah. They view their Creator as vengeful and ever ready to punish and live their lives in total fear of making the smallest error. But this is not the Islamic perspective of the Creator.

Islam teaches us to have a healthy, balanced attitude towards the Creator. Our relationship with Allah must be grounded in the love of Allah. We must learn His Beautiful Names and Attributes and recognize His Blessings in our lives. This should make us fall in love with the Creator. When we love the Creator, we will want to submit to Him and obey Him.

Reflect on the following attributes of Allah. He is Perfect in every way. His perfection extends beyond our imagination in ways we cannot understand. He is the Most Merciful (al-Rahman), Perfectly Compassionate (al-Rahim), Most Loving (al-Wadud), Most Forgiving (al-Ghafur), the Acceptor of Repentance (al-Tawwab), and so much more.

Building on this love is a balance of hope and fear. Out of love of Allah, we hope for His Mercy when we slip up, and we never despair of Allah's Forgiveness. He is Most Merciful, Most Forgiving. But also, because we love Him so much, we fear displeasing Him and not worshipping Him as He deserves. This fear keeps us away from sins and pushes us to repent whenever we slip up.

Developing a healthy balance between hope and fear, rooted in love, is necessary for having a good relationship with the Creator. When your thoughts about Allah are positive, you live your life with more optimism, happiness, and inner peace. You know that Allah is protecting you and will take care of you, and this helps you through the difficult stages of life, too.

Fix your perspective on your Creator by studying His Names and Attributes. When you rediscover His Majesty and Glory, and love Him for His Perfection, then you will find inner peace and true happiness. Real happiness begins by fixing your relationship with the One who matters most: your Creator. Allah created us to worship Him, so let us worship Him in the best ways possible, and let that worship be our means of attaining true happiness.

KEY FIVE

ACCEPT THAT
LIFE IS A TEST

إِنَّا جَعَلْنَا مَا عَلَى الْأَرْضِ زِينَةً لَهَا لِنَبْلُوَهُمْ أَيُّهُمْ أَحْسَنُ عَمَلًا

وَإِنَّا لَجَاعِلُونَ مَا عَلَيْهَا صَعِيدًا جُرُزًا

Innaa ja'alnaa ma 'alal ardi zeenatal lahaa
linabluwahum ayyuhum ahsanu 'amalaa. Wa innaa
la jaa'iloona maa 'alaihaa sa'eedan juruzaa

We have indeed made whatever is on earth beautiful
for it, in order to test which of them is best in deeds.
And We will certainly reduce whatever is on it to
barren ground (Surah al-Kahf 18:7–8)

Life is a test. It is not meant to be easy all the time.
Paradise is the place of eternal rest and ease, but to
get there, we must be tested, and we must pass the
various tests of life. Once we accept that life is a test,
it becomes easier to deal with reality and to have realistic expectations of life.

Islam does not promise us a life of ease, wealth, and success if we choose the straight path. The prosperity gospel is not an Islamic teaching. The prosperity gospel refers to the modern misconception that piety will lead to riches and a pain-free life. Although this belief is quite popular today, it is not what Islam teaches us.

Rather, we are taught that every believer will be tested in a variety of ways to determine who is truly sincere. The key to unlocking eternal happiness is to handle the tests of life in a way that is pleasing to Allah.

The Qur'an is full of reminders that life is a test.

وَلَنَبْلُوَنَّكُمْ بِشَيْءٍ مِنَ الْخَوْفِ وَالْجُوعِ وَنَقْصٍ مِنَ الْأَمْوَالِ

وَالْأَنْفُسِ وَالثَّمَرَاتِ وَبَشِّرِ الصَّابِرِينَ

الَّذِينَ إِذَا أَصَابَتْهُمْ مُصِيبَةٌ قَالُوا إِنَّا لِلَّهِ وَإِنَّا إِلَيْهِ رَاجِعُونَ

Wa lanablu wannakum bishai'im minal khawfi waljoo'i wa naqsim minal amwaali wal anfusi was samaraati; wa bashshiris saabireen Allazeena izaaa asaabathum museebatun qaalooo innaa lillaahi wa innaaa ilaihi raaji'oon

We will test you with some kind of fear and hunger, and loss of wealth, lives, and fruit. So, give glad tidings to those who are patient, those who when afflicted with calamity say to God we belong and to Him we will return
(Surah al-Baqarah 2:155–156)

أَحَسِبَ النَّاسُ أَنْ يُتْرَكُوا أَنْ يَقُولُوا آمَنَّا وَهُمْ لَا يُفْتَنُونَ

وَلَقَدْ فَتَنَّا الَّذِينَ مِنْ قَبْلِهِمْ فَلَيَعْلَمَنَّ اللَّهُ الَّذِينَ صَدَقُوا

وَلَيَعْلَمَنَّ الْكَاذِبِينَ

*Ahasiban naasu any yutrakooo any yaqoolooo
aamannaa wa hum la yuftanoon*

*Wa laqad fatannal lazeena min qablihim fala
ya'lamannal laahul lazeena sadaqoo wa la
ya'lamannal kaazibeen*

**Do people think that they will be left upon saying
we believe and that they will not be tested? We have
definitely tested those before them, so that Allah can
make known the truthful and the liars
(Surah al-Ankabut 29:2–3)**

This message is repeated in various hadiths, as the
Prophet ﷺ warned us that the most severely tested
people are those who are closest to God, and each
person is tested according to their level of faith. (Tirmidhi 2398)

If life is a test, does this mean that we can never be
happy? The Prophet ﷺ was tested more than any other
human, yet he remained a pleasant, joyful person to
be around. Despite losing most of his family, being
exiled, slandered, and having to fight battles against
his own tribe, he never developed a bitter personality.
He ﷺ is our model of true Islamic happiness. He ﷺ
taught us that no matter what trials we face in life

we can still find happiness and inner peace by having a strong connection with our Creator.

When we accept the world as it is, we will have more realistic expectations. In that case, we will not attach our happiness to material possessions or fame or amassing a lot of wealth. We will be content and happy with what Allah provides us with and will find joy in the little things in life. Life is a test, but if we learn to accept our destiny, then we can pass the test with an A grade.

TURN TO ALLAH IN TIMES OF EASE AND DIFFICULTY

The Messenger ﷺ said, "Be mindful of Allah, and you will find Him in front of you. Recognize and acknowledge Allah in times of ease and prosperity, and He will remember you in times of adversity. And know that what has passed you by [and you have failed to attain] was not going to befall you, and what has befallen you was not going to pass you by. And know that victory comes with patience, relief with affliction, and hardship with ease."

(Tirmidhi 2516)

Life goes through various phases of ups and downs. For many people, this means facing periods of ease and periods of difficulty. A key to maintaining your inner peace and composure during times of difficulty is to remain committed to Allah during both phases of life.

True believers worship Allah wholeheartedly, regardless of how good or bad life gets. They do not let the trials of life distract them from the ultimate purpose which is the worship of the Creator. Nor do they allow wealth and success to distract them from their true purpose. In both situations, the believer remains focused on living a life that is pleasing to Allah. When a person does this, they will find inner peace even during the darkest of times.

Allah assists His believers during difficult times in many ways. This may include answered prayers and miracles, or other ways in which Allah's Divine assistance manifests, such as feelings of optimism and inner peace, true dreams, ease in other aspects of life, or experiencing a lot of personal growth through the trials. Allah's assistance comes in many ways.

Many who lived like this can testify that even during their darkest trials, they experienced a closeness to Allah. In fact, it may be the closest they ever felt to Allah, and the trial later becomes a fond memory of an event that brought them closer to Him and shaped their lives and personalities. Therefore, for the believer, even hardship and trials can be blessings when they are approached with commitment to Allah and a firm belief that Allah knows what is best for us.

TREAT YOUR PARENTS WELL

وَقَضَىٰ رَبُّكَ أَلَّا تَعْبُدُوا إِلَّا إِيَّاهُ وَبِالْوَالِدَيْنِ إِحْسَانًا إِمَّا يَبْلُغَنَّ عِنْدَكَ الْكِبَرَ أَحَدُهُمَا أَوْ كِلَاهُمَا فَلَا تَقُلْ لَهُمَا أُفٍّ وَلَا تَنْهَرْهُمَا وَقُلْ لَهُمَا قَوْلًا كَرِيمًا

Wa qadaa Rabbuka allaa ta'budooo illaaa iyyaahu wa bilwaalidaini ihsaanaa immaa yablughanna 'indakal kibara ahaduhumaaa aw kilaahumaa falaa taqul lahumaaa uffinw wa laa tanharhumaa wa qullahumaa qawlan kareemaa

And your Lord has decreed that you worship not except Him, and to treat your parents well. Whether one or both of them reach old age with you, do not say a bad word to them and do not rebuke them but speak to them kindly (Surah al-Isra 17:23)

Your parents are your pathway to Paradise. It is through them that Allah brought you into this world, and it is in serving them that you will find inner peace and a path to Paradise and forgiveness. Parents are often an unappreciated gift from Allah until they are gone, but it does not have to be that way. Appreciate them now, cherish them, spend quality time with them, make them smile, and benefit from their wisdom. One day, your parents will return to your Lord. Make sure you have done everything you can before that to make them happy.

Modern society tends to downplay the importance of parents. The media portrays parents as backwards and stupid and encourages us to abandon them in favour of our own desires. It teaches that we do not owe our parents anything and that they just did what they had to do. This toxic culture has resulted in pain, loneliness, and sadness for all involved. Parents experience the pain and loneliness of abandonment in their old age, whilst their children experience a regret that cannot be healed once their parents have passed away.

Islam teaches us that our parents have the most rights over us after God and His Messenger. Many hadiths encourage us to be kind to our parents and remind us that the blessings of Allah in both worlds can be found in the kind treatment of one's parents, especially when they reach old age. Caring for one's parents in old age is considered one of the greatest deeds a person can do, and one of the quickest paths to earning Allah's forgiveness.

The famous companion Abdullah ibn 'Umar ﷺ said, "The pleasure of the Lord lies in the pleasure of the parent. The anger of the Lord lies in the anger of the parent." (al-Adab al-Mufrad, 2)

On another occasion, he advised a man to care for his elderly mother as atonement for his sins. He told him "By Allah, if you speak gently to her and feed her, then you will enter the Garden as long as you avoid the major sins." (al-Adab al-Mufrad, 8)

On another occasion, Ibn 'Umar ﷺ saw a Yemeni man making tawaf of the Kabah while carrying his mother on his back, saying, "I am your humble camel. If her mount is frightened, I am not frightened." Then he asked, "Ibn 'Umar? Do you think that I have repaid her?" Ibn 'Umar replied, "No, not even for a single groan (of labour pain)." (al-Adab al-Mufrad, 11)

Parents occupy a high and special status in Islam. Nothing we do can make up for the sacrifices a mother makes when taking care of her young baby or the long hours a father spends working hard to provide for his children. But if we show gratitude and treat them well then we will experience peace, blessings, and forgiveness through these noble acts. Our happiness is linked to the pleasure of Allah, and Allah is pleased with the one who makes his parents smile.

MAINTAIN FAMILY TIES

يَا أَيُّهَا النَّاسُ اتَّقُوا رَبَّكُمُ الَّذِي خَلَقَكُم مِّن نَّفْسٍ وَاحِدَةٍ وَخَلَقَ مِنْهَا زَوْجَهَا وَبَثَّ مِنْهُمَا رِجَالًا كَثِيرًا وَنِسَاءً ۚ وَاتَّقُوا اللَّهَ الَّذِي تَسَاءَلُونَ بِهِ وَالْأَرْحَامَ ۚ إِنَّ اللَّهَ كَانَ عَلَيْكُمْ رَقِيبًا

Yaaa aiyuhan naasut taqoo Rabbakumul lazee khalaqakum min nafsinw waahidatinw wa khalaqa minhaa zawjahaa wa bas sa minhumaa rijaalan kaseeranw wa nisaaa'aa; wattaqul laahallazee tasaaa 'aloona bihee wal arhaam; innal laaha kaana 'alaikum Raqeeba

O people! Fear your Lord, who created you from a single soul, and created from it its mate, and propagated from them many men and women. And revere God whom you ask about, and the parents. Surely, God is Watchful over you (Surah al-Nisa 4:1)

The Messenger ﷺ said, "Whoever believes in Allah and the Last Day, let him uphold his family ties." (Sahih al-Bukhari 6138)

27

We all need family. Not just our spouses and children, but the whole clan. We need good relationships with our parents, siblings, uncles, aunts, cousins, and grandparents. The more family relationships you can juggle well, the more meaningful life becomes. Allah created us in families because strong family ties are what is best for us.

Hyper-individualism has killed family ties. People care only about themselves and do not seek out meaningful relationships, even with their own siblings. They think that they do not need anyone else, and all they need is to fulfil their own desires. They slowly alienate their entire families and become lonesome creatures focused only on self-gratification. There is no real happiness in such self-imposed isolation. We were created to be families, tribes, and communities, not to be selfish and live alone.

Maintaining family ties is an important act of worship in Islam. Severing a relationship with any family member without a just cause is a major sin. A Muslim, therefore, cannot ignore this important dynamic. Our families are our protection against outside threats. Without family, we are vulnerable in more ways than we can imagine.

When the Prophet Lut ﷺ was sent to call his people away from sexual deviancies back to the straight path, he did not have strong family support.

قَالَ لَوْ أَنَّ لِي بِكُمْ قُوَّةً أَوْ آوِي إِلَىٰ رُكْنٍ شَدِيدٍ

Qaala law anna lee bikum quwwatan aw aaweee ilaa ruknin shadeed

He lamented, "If only I had the strength to stop you or could rely on some strong support (Surah Hud 11:80)

Without the support of a tribe or strong family, Prophet Lut ﷺ was unable to physically fight his people. Eventually, Allah destroyed the city and saved him and his family, besides his wife, who was also destroyed for supporting their sexual sins.

Compare this to the final Prophet ﷺ who was born into a strong and noble family. In the early years of Islam, many of his enemies wanted to attack and even kill him. One thing that held them back from doing so was his family. The Prophet's ﷺ tribe mostly protected him, even those who did not believe him. This shows the importance of building a strong powerful family. Our families are our first defence against the outside world.

Do not neglect family relationships. Spend quality time with your parents, children, spouses, siblings, grandparents, and extended family. The amount of time you spend with them will differ based on how close you are, but at the very least, try to spend quality time daily with your immediate family, and once a week with extended family.

There are great blessings in maintaining family ties, which include being blessed with a long life and abundant sustenance. The Prophet ﷺ said, "Anyone who wants to have his provision expanded and his term of life prolonged should maintain ties of kinship." (Sahih al-Bukhari 2067)

I have personally witnessed in my life many people who strived to maintain family ties, and in return, were blessed with long lives and abundant wealth, despite being born into adverse situations.

Strong family ties are crucial for a happy life. Our families can be a primary source of happiness for us or the first enemy that makes our lives miserable. If we strive to maintain family ties, then we are rewarded regardless of whether others respond in kind. In most situations, however, the fruit of maintaining family ties is the development of strong blood relationships that will benefit all involved for the rest of their lives.

The Messenger ﷺ said, "Whoever believes in Allah and the Last Day, let him uphold his family ties."

(Sahih al-Bukhari 6138)

BE YOUR SPOUSE'S SOURCE OF PEACE

وَمِنْ آيَاتِهِ أَنْ خَلَقَ لَكُمْ مِنْ أَنْفُسِكُمْ أَزْوَاجًا لِتَسْكُنُوا إِلَيْهَا وَجَعَلَ بَيْنَكُمْ مَوَدَّةً وَرَحْمَةً إِنَّ فِي ذَٰلِكَ لَآيَاتٍ لِقَوْمٍ يَتَفَكَّرُونَ

Wa min Aayaatiheee an khalaqa lakum min anfusikum azwaajal litaskunooo ilaihaa wa ja'ala bainakum mawad datanw wa rahmah; inna fee zaalika la Aayaatil liqawminy yatafakkaroon

And one of His signs is that He created for you spouses from among yourselves so that you may find comfort in them. And He has placed between you compassion and mercy. Surely in this are signs for people who reflect (Surah al-Rum 30:21)

One of the greatest sources of joy in this world is a righteous, loving spouse. The Prophet ﷺ said, "Everything in this world is a source of enjoyment, and the greatest source of enjoyment is a righteous spouse." (Sahih Muslim 1467)

31

Allah created men and women for each other. When love develops between husband and wife, it forms a powerful bond that makes their relationship a true blessing. This relationship is strong enough to power you through some of life's greatest trials.

One of the goals of marriage in Islam is to have someone in your life who is your primary source of peace and joy. Other goals of marriage include protection of chastity, producing offspring, experiencing love, and access to halal intimacy. All these goals are important, and both spouses must strive to assist each other in achieving these goals throughout their relationship.

The word used in the above verse is *taskunu*, which has its root in *Sakina*. *Sakina* refers to tranquillity or inner peace, and this means that our homes should be places in which we feel peace and tranquillity, a refuge from the outside world and all its trials.

There are many ways we can be that source of peace for our spouses. Both spouses need to work on this for it to flourish, and a one-sided effort can often result in frustration and resentment. Make it a priority in your life to make your spouse smile and laugh.

When both men and women understand the needs of the opposite gender and go out of their way to please their spouses, the result is a powerful, joyful relationship that brings peace and happiness to both their souls. Marriage requires investment of time and effort, but the results are worth it. There are very few things in this world that can produce happiness on the same level as a strong, loving marriage.

One of the strongest benefits of marriage is having someone to face the challenges of life with. Together, you are more capable of getting through the highs and lows of life. When people work together, they are able to accomplish so much more. This applies especially to a marriage.

Couples should look at their marriages as their most important alliance. When this alliance is strong, there is no trial too big for you to overcome. Investing in your marriage is investing in your own happiness.

KEY TEN

CHERISH EVERY MOMENT WITH YOUR CHILDREN

Al-Aqra' ibn Habis saw the Prophet ﷺ kissing his grandson Al-Hasan. He said, "I have ten children and I do not kiss any of them." The Prophet ﷺ said, "Verily, whoever does not show mercy will not receive mercy."

(Sahih al-Bukhari 5997 & Sahih Muslim 2318)

Children are a gift and trust from Allah. Every child that Allah blesses a couple with is a gift. You are trusted to raise that child in a way that is pleasing to Allah so that they grow up to worship Allah and become assets to the ummah.

Allah decides who can have children and what children they can have. He tests some with infertility and gives some only boys, others only girls, and some he gifts with both. Every family should be grateful to Allah for what He gives them, because only Allah knows what is best for us in the long run.

Our children grow up faster than we realize. The time they spend in our homes is very short compared to the length of their lives if Allah blesses them with long lives. Someone who lives in this world for seventy years tends to spend only the first fifteen to twenty years in their parents' home. The rest of their life is spent as an adult fulfilling their duties towards Allah and His Creation.

Those twenty years go by very quickly. Too often, we are so distracted by our work, trials, and life that we fail to spend quality time with our children. Not only does this affect the child's development and attachment to their parents, but it also leads to regret when parents realize that it is too late to enjoy childhood memories, as their children have already grown up.

The goal of parenting is to raise men and women who will worship Allah, serve His religion, and be productive members of society. To fulfil this goal, we must develop strong relationships with our children. Strong relationships are built on spending quality time with them and expressing one's love for them.

The Prophet ﷺ lived in a culture in which it was considered unmasculine for a man to show affection to his children. He practically demonstrated to people that this idea was false. The Prophet ﷺ was the most loving of fathers, grandfathers, and stepfathers. He treated all children with love and care.

He would honour his daughter Fatima ﵂ whenever she would visit his home, and he would carry, hug, kiss, and play with his grandchildren in public so that people could see a practical example of a loving father. He gave special attention to his wives' children from previous marriages so that they never felt deprived of fatherly love. He demonstrated for us the perfect role model of a loving father.

Children need love and affection to grow confident, strong, and mature. They need to know their parents love them, believe in them, and want what is best for them. This inspires them to grow up quickly and become the best versions of themselves.

Your children will leave your home sooner than you think. Do not be distracted by work and trials from building strong relationships with your children. Spend quality time with them. Teach them the religion and good character. Enjoy hobbies together. Build memories together. You will find yourself at your happiest during these moments.

MAKE TIME FOR YOURSELF TOO

The Messenger ﷺ said, "Fear Allah for your family has rights over you and your guest has rights over you. Verily, your own self has rights over you, so fast and break your fast, pray and sleep."

(Abu Dawud 1369)

t is so easy to get lost in our obligations and responsibilities. If we go too hard into trying to please everyone else, we may end up neglecting ourselves. Balance requires making time for yourself, too. If you have done justice to worship, work, and family time, then there should be no guilt in enjoying some quality alone time or indulging in a halal recreational activity.

The soul also needs rest and recovery. Nobody can work all the time without relaxation and remain sane and productive. Our bodies need sleep, healthy food, and downtime. The rules of Islam are realistic and accommodate for the human need for rest and recreation. Anything that humans naturally need have their place in Islam.

Islam does not prohibit fun or relaxation. It simply

teaches us to keep every activity in its place. Modern culture prioritizes fun over everything else. Many people delay marriage or having children because they fear it will get in the way of their fun. Some people delay growing up and remain children for life because they do not want to let go of their fun, nor do they want any responsibilities. This unhealthy pattern has led to loneliness, lack of purpose, and depression for many. Humans were not created to remain children for life or only indulge in fun. Our lives are meant for a deeper purpose.

The other extreme is people who shun all types of fun as unproductive or unislamic. They assume that being a good Muslim means being serious and harsh all the time, and never enjoying the good things of this world. Both extremes are far away from the understanding of the early generations. The early Muslims were responsible adults who prioritized their work, worship, and family responsibilities. But they also enjoyed halal fun and did not see it as unislamic or counterproductive.

The early Muslims would race with their horses, swim, wrestle, joke with each other, write poetry, and sing wholesome songs about faith and life. Over time, Muslims developed other past times like board games and hanging out at coffee shops. None of these things are prohibited in Islam if done in moderation.

Happiness requires balance, and part of balance is taking care of yourself. Do not feel guilty about having a personal hobby or pastime that helps you relax and recharge for the next day of work. This is part of fulfilling the rights of your own body upon you and is necessary for living a happy life.

SPEND TIME IN GOOD COMPANY

The Messenger ﷺ said, "A man follows the religion of his friend; everyone should be careful about whom he takes as his close friend."

(Abu Dawud 4833)

Our friends can be our biggest source of joy or sorrow in this world. Good company can bring a smile to your face and fill your life with good memories. Bad company can lead to betrayals and heartache of the worst kind. Our friends shape our personalities. We often inherit the traits of those who we are closest to. In this way, choosing your friend circle is crucial for deciding the kind of person you want to become.

Good company refers to real friends. A true friend is someone who cares about you spiritually. They will not encourage you to sin or distract you from worshipping Allah. They will travel the paths of Islam with you. A good friend is not perfect, because nobody is, but a good friend tries their best and encourages you to try, too.

Good friends also care about you in this world. Your pain is their pain, and your success makes them happy. Their advice is genuine and sincere. Their love is pure and for the sake of Allah. They make time for you and want to see your success in both worlds. They are people you can rely on for support at times of trial and tragedy.

Bad company are people who do not care about your Afterlife and may even seek to destroy it. Insincere friends take joy in your failures and are jealous when you succeed. They are around you when they need something and forget about you during your time of need. They are selfish and materialistic, caring only about this world and worldly success. You are an after-thought to them, and they only like you to the level that you can benefit them. Their care is not real, and they will betray you in a heartbeat.

To attract good friends into our lives, we must become good company. We must be the true friend to others and search for them in places of righteousness. Friend ships is mutually beneficial relationships because the love and care between friends are mutual. Seek out good company and invest your time in developing these relationships. Over time, you will find what you are looking for, and your friends will become a pri mary source of happiness for you.

BE A PART OF YOUR COMMUNITY

The Messenger ﷺ said, "The believer who mixes with people and is patient with their harm has a greater reward than the believer who does not mix with people, nor is patient with their harm."

(Ibn Majah 4032)

Humans are social creatures. We are not meant to be alone forever. While we may find peace and happiness in solitude, it is only valuable when it is part of a healthy lifestyle. Being alone all the time can lead to depression and feelings of loneliness. We were meant to be part of a community, and a lot of our success lies in doing so.

Sometimes we do not want to be part of the broader community. We worry about bad influences, betrayal, and the harm others may cause us. None of this should stop us from becoming part of the community, however, as all of this is part of the human experience and necessary for our growth. Without experiencing the highs and lows of community life, we cannot gain wisdom.

The modern world has become hyper-individualistic. In such cultures, people seem to care only about themselves, with no concern for the broader community. They ignore their immediate family, have no clue who their neighbours are, and have no relationship with the community at large. This leads to isolation, depression, and a variety of mental health problems. All this can be avoided if we learn to value our communities.

Start with the local masjid or Islamic centre. Begin frequenting these places and forming relationships with others there. Build these relationships and find ways to serve the community. Volunteer your time and skills for projects that benefit the broader community and utilize your income to fund these projects.

Over time, you will learn to value and appreciate your community, and will find joy in service. This joy cannot be experienced when focused only on yourself—you need to get out there and be part of the community. Do so, and your life will be more meaningful and satisfying.

LIVE A LIFE OF CONTRIBUTION

The Messenger ﷺ said, "Whoever relieves a Muslim of a burden from the burdens of the world, Allah will relieve him of a burden from the burdens on the Day of Judgement. And whoever helps ease a difficulty in the world, Allah will grant him ease from a difficulty in the world and in the Hereafter."

(Tirmidhi 1930)

Do not live a selfish existence. Make time daily to serve others. Even if you cannot find a job or career that allows you to be of service, dedicate some of your free time to helping others. In serving others, we experience a deeper sense of happiness and inner peace that cannot be explained. It is a happiness that Allah blesses the hearts of the generous with.

Even modern psychologists have prescribed community service as one of the many ways of fighting depression. Its effects on the heart and the ability to replace sadness with happiness and contentment are clear for anyone to see. If you have been living in isolation, focused only on your own desire, yet still feel empty and sad inside, perhaps it is time to go out and be part of the community again.

There are many ways to serve the community. The easiest is to donate online to various causes around the globe. This is noble and highly encouraged, but I would suggest going beyond this. There is more benefit in physically being involved and witnessing the trials others go through. It is good to donate to an orphanage online, but it is even better to visit an orphanage, talk to the orphans, and spend time with them in person. This approach will have a far deeper effect on your heart than simply donating from afar.

Try to make time to be part of the community and to interact with those members of your community that need you most. Visit an orphanage, volunteer at your local masjid or Islamic centre, host a meal for the poor, be a part of your community, and be a source of ease for them during their difficult times.

When you serve the community, many beautiful things happen. You will develop a deeper sense of appreciation for what you have. Your own problems become trivialized in comparison to others. You may form deep friendships with the people you serve, help and work with. You will feel happier and more optimistic about your life. And you will unlock a Divine assistance in your own life. Allah takes special care of those who care about others. Dedicate a portion of your time to make life easier for others, and Allah will take special care of you and your family, too.

BE SATISFIED WITH A HARD DAY'S WORK

The Messenger of Allah ﷺ said, "By him in whose hand is my soul, if one of you were to carry a bundle of firewood on his back and sell it, that would be better for him than begging a man who may or may not give him anything."

(Sahih al-Bukhari 1401 & Sahih Muslim 1042)

Earning halal is important; we need to work hard and earn well enough to provide good lives for our families. This protects us from a lot of trials that come with poverty, while giving us extra that can be spent in the path of Allah. However, obsession with high profits can cloud one's judgment. The desire to always get more and more can distract us from the blessings we already have. It may be that we are doing fine, we have everything we need, and life is beautiful, but we do not recognize any of this because our eye is always on the next profit goal.

Although Muslims should work hard and strive to be productive providers for their families, our sustenance is not entirely in our hands. Allah instructs us to strive for our sustenance, but also informs us that He is the Provider, and He provides us according to what is best for our souls. At times, this may not be what we want in terms of wealth. If excessive wealth might corrupt our souls, then Allah may protect us from that by keeping our profit margins low.

Our happiness should not be attached to how well we earn. The exact amount of earnings is a matter of destiny and is outside our control. In our control is our ability to work hard and try our best. It is in this that we should take pride and find joy. Work hard, try your best, give it your all, and then be satisfied with what Allah has provided you for the day. This is a healthier and ultimately happier, way to handle our work lives.

"Be moderate in seeking from the world, for everyone will be facilitated towards what has been decreed for him in it." (Al-Bayhaqi, 10501)

"Were the son of Adam to flee from his provision as he flees from death, his provision would surely reach him just as death will reach him."

(Hilyatul al-Awliya, 7:90)

SEEK PROTECTION FROM POVERTY

اللَّهُمَّ إِنِّي أَعُوذُ بِكَ مِنَ الْفَقْرِ وَالْقِلَّةِ وَالذَّلَّةِ وَأَعُوذُ بِكَ مِنْ أَنْ
أَظْلِمَ أَوْ أُظْلَمَ

Allahumma innee a'udhubika minal faqri walqillati wazzillati wa a'uzubika min an azlima aw uzlam.

The Messenger ﷺ said, "O Allah, I seek refuge in You from poverty, scarcity, and humiliation. I seek refuge in You from committing wrong or being wronged." (Abu Dawud 1544)

A misconception many Muslims have is that poverty is glorified in Islam. This is incorrect. The Prophet ﷺ taught us several prayers in which we seek protection from poverty. If poverty was something desirable, he would not have taught us to make such prayers.

Wealth and poverty are both tests from Allah. He tests different people with different tests, and many He tests with both at different stages of their lives. Poverty is a test that we should seek protection from and actively strive against by developing a strong work ethic and trying our best every day to earn well.

Poverty makes a person vulnerable to sin and temptation. When desperate, people may turn to various sinful means to earn some income or get some food. They may steal or sell their bodies in desperation. We ask Allah to protect us from such situations and to keep us far away from such poverty.

Our sustenance is written by Allah, but we do not know what is written for us and must seek it with a good effort. True believers work hard and strive to become financially independent. They do not desire poverty, but rather desire halal wealth that can be used in a way that is pleasing to Allah. To achieve this, they work hard and try their best every day, and thank Allah at the end of each day for what He has provided them with.

When praying to Allah, actively seek protection from poverty by including these recommended prayers in your daily supplications:

اللّهُـمَّ اكْفِـني بِحَلالِـلِكَ عَنْ حَـرامِـك، وَأَغْنِـني بِفَضْـلِكَ عَمَّـنْ سِـواك

Allahummakfinee bihalaalika an haraamik,
wa aghnini bi fadlika amman siwaak.

O Allah, suffice me with what You have allowed instead of what You have forbidden, and make me independent of all others besides You.
(Tirmidhi 3563)

اللّٰهُمَّ إِنِّي أَعُوذُ بِكَ مِنَ الهَمِّ وَ الْحُـزْنِ والعَجْـزِ والكَسَلِ
والبُخْلِ والْجُبْنِ، وضَلْـعِ الـدَّيْنِ وغَلَبَـةِ الرِّجال

Allahumma innee a'oodhu bika minal-hammi wal-huzni, wal-ajzi wal-kasali, wal-bukhli wal-jubni, wa dal'id-dayn, wa ghalabatir-rijaal.

**O Allah! I seek refuge with You from worry and grief, from incapacity and laziness, from cowardice and miserliness, from being heavily in debt and from being overpowered by (other) men.
(Sahih al-Bukhari 6369)**

اللّٰهُـمَّ إِنِّـي أَعــوذُبِكَ مِنَ الْكُـفر، وَالفَـقْـر، وَأَعــوذُ بِكَ مِنْ
عَـذابِ القَـبْرِ، لا إلٰهَ إلاَّ أَنْـتَ

Allahumma innee a'oodhu bika minal-kufri, wal-faqri, wa a'oodhu bika min adhaabil-qabr, laa ilaaha illa ant.

O Allah, I seek refuge in You from disbelief and poverty, and I seek refuge in You from the punishment of the grave. There is none worthy of worship but You. (Abu Dawud 5090)

ENSURE YOUR FOOD AND WEALTH ARE HALAL

The Messenger ﷺ once mentioned a parable of a man who, having journeyed far, is dishevelled and dusty, and who spreads out his hands to the sky saying "O Lord! O Lord!" while his food is haram (unlawful), his drink is haram, his clothing is haram, and he has been nourished with haram, so how can his supplication be answered?

(Sahih Muslim 1015)

A blessed life is a life funded through halal means. Whether you choose to live simple or live a life of luxury within your means, the key is to keep it halal. Your sources of income, purchases, and possessions should all be halal. These days there is a lot of obsession over meat being halal, but not enough focus on the wealth that we purchase that meat with also being halal.

Muslims must be concerned with their sources of income. A small amount of halal income that covers the basics and keeps your family together is more blessed than large amounts of haram income. Haram income brings with it the wrath of Allah and many spiritual problems. A Muslim cannot afford to neglect this aspect of life. Halal income is not a luxury but a necessity.

Choose a career or trade that is clearly permissible and avoid any dodgy sources of income. Try your best to avoid interest-based transactions by seeking halal alternatives. Live within your means and avoid falling into debt. Ensure that you purchase your food from halal outlets and that the clothing you wear is halal, too. These issues should always be a priority for a Muslim and should never be neglected.

When you prioritize halal, amazing things happen. Your spiritual state increases as you find yourself getting closer to Allah, even through your work and purchases. This is because you are always thinking about Allah and what is pleasing to Him, even when working or shopping. Your family will more likely grow up to be righteous because their homes, food, clothes, and income are halal, and the blessing of this includes righteous offspring. Furthermore, your prayers will be answered, because Allah does not usually answer the prayers of someone who earns haram. Prioritize halal, and you will find your life full of blessings, contentment, and inner peace.

BE CONTENT WITH ENOUGH

The Messenger ﷺ said, "Wealth is not in having many possessions. Rather, true wealth is the contentment of the soul."

(Sahih al-Bukhari 6446 & Sahih Muslim 1051)

The opposite of poverty is also a trial. Too much wealth can open the doors of temptation and distract a person from the worship of Allah. It takes a strong disciplined soul to remain committed to the obedi ence of Allah when the door of every temptation is easily accessible.

The wealth of this world is a double-edged sword. For some people, it is a blessing that they spend in the path of Allah. It is a means through which they earn Paradise and benefit society. For others, it is a door of temptation that allows them to access sins that were previously closed to them.

Greed is something that has no limits. A wealthy person can always find someone who has more than them, or another milestone to meet in piling up their wealth. The Prophet ﷺ said, "If the son of Adam had a valley full of gold, he would want to have two valleys. Nothing fills his mouth but the dust of the grave, yet Allah will relent to whoever repents to Him." (Sahih al-Bukhari 6439)

Recognizing that greed has no limits and how easy it is to become obsessed with always having more, it is important to figure out what is sufficient for us. Each family and individual is unique in this regard, but we all can determine what is sufficient to meet our needs.

Figure out how much wealth you need to be independent, happy, and comfortable, and work towards that goal. If Allah blesses you with enough, then think carefully about your next goal in life. For some people, earning more will open more doors of good deeds so they seek out more wealth to spend in the path of Allah.

For others, excessive wealth may corrupt them or their families, and it may be better to stop and be content with what Allah has given. This is a decision that everyone must make based on what is best for their souls and their families' souls. Protecting the spirituality of the family, and their connection to Allah, should take precedence over amassing wealth.

The truth is that most of us do not need that much to live happy, content lives. If you take the time to do the math, you may realize it is a much more achievable number than you realize. Once you figure it out, work towards earning that amount of wealth, then be content. Chasing a second valley of gold could open the doors of greed and distract you from enjoying what you already have.

DO NOT SEEK WHAT OTHERS HAVE

The Messenger ﷺ said, "Renounce the worldly life and Allah will love you. Renounce what people possess, and people will love you."

(Ibn Majah 4102)

Jealousy destroys any semblance of happiness and fills the heart with bitterness. When people are constantly focused on the blessings of others that they do not have, they become unable to see the good in their own lives, and the desire to have what others have consumes them.

A key to happiness is to be satisfied with what Allah has given you and to be pleased for others when Allah blesses them. Our sustenance is decreed by Allah, and He decides who will receive which blessings based on His Infinite Wisdom. It may be that what is a blessing for someone else may be a source of misguidance for you, so Allah protected you from that by not giving you that same item.

We must learn to look at the things of this world through the lens of destiny. Everything in this world belongs to Allah, and He tests each of us with different types of gifts and trials. Some people have many children but are tested with their children's personalities. Others may struggle to have children but are gifted with just one that is the coolness of their eyes. Some are gifted many children, all of whom are the coolness of their eyes, but struggle with finances or health issues instead. Each person's gifts and trials are different. We must learn to accept our destiny and appreciate it.

There are various levels of piety related to accepting destiny. The lowest is to be patient with one's destiny. This means that you may not like the position you are in, but you are patient with it for the sake of Allah. Higher than this is contentment. Contentment means that although you desire more, you are satisfied with what Allah has blessed you with.

The highest level is to be pleased with one's destiny. This is the rank of the true friends of Allah, and the key to a life of happiness. The righteous know that whatever Allah wills for them is best for them, so they are pleased with their destiny, even in situations that cause others depression and grief. At this level, the problems of this world cannot cause them any grief. They are content, happy, and love whatever Allah loves. Reaching this level is not necessary for salvation or happiness, but it is a truly remarkable achievement if one reaches it.

PRACTICE GOOD MANNERS

THE MESSENGER ﷺ SAID, "NOTHING IS HEAVIER ON THE SCALE OF DEEDS THAN ONE'S GOOD MANNERS."

(TIRMIDHI 2002)

A lot of our problems stem from our own manners and ways of interacting. What we perceive as the anger and emotional outbursts of others are often just reactions to our own harshness, coarseness, and rudeness. To fix our dealings with others, we must look inward and reflect on our own manners.

Manners are an important part of Islam. Entire books are written about the topic, and even entire chapters of the Qur'an were revealed about it. The Prophet ﷺ is our model of perfect manners. His Sunnah needs to be studied and analysed to deduce the best of manners. To become truly well-mannered, we must become people of the Sunnah.

There are many aspects of manners that are key to happiness in a social context. It begins with greeting people but extends to honesty, trustworthiness, integrity, kindness, generosity, and general politeness. These acts of good manners may seem insignificant, but they weigh heavily on the scale on the Last Day and go a long way towards building strong relationships in this world.

Think about this. Which type of person would you prefer to befriend? The rough, harsh, vulgar, untrustworthy, arrogant jerk, or the kind, polite, well-spoken, honest, humble hero? Be the second type of person, and that is the kind of friend circle you will end up building around you.

When we live with others in a well-mannered way, we stop many arguments before they ever happen and become models of peace and kindness for others. In this way, many of the obstacles to happiness can be averted, and happiness can naturally take its course. I have never met someone who said that being well-mannered has led to unhappiness. Have you?

MAINTAIN GOOD CHARACTER

The Messenger ﷺ said, "I have been sent to perfect good character."

(Al-Muwatta 1614)

The difference between manners and character is the difference between the external and internal. Manners are how we interact with others; character is what is in our hearts during those interactions. Manners can be faked, character cannot. Part of the prophetic mission was to model good character for us.

Attaining good character requires reflection and constant purification of the soul. It means facing our inner demons and defeating them. This is an ongoing battle, but each victory is sweet. The alternative is falling into darkness and becoming the worst version of ourselves.

Good character and bad character are opposite that exist in the heart. Each of these comes in pairs Humility and arrogance, sincerity and hypocrisy love and hatred, empathy and enmity, altruism and jealousy. A key to happiness is to reflect on one's own spiritual state and to replace each negative characteristic with its pure opposite.

Fundamentals of good character include being sincere to Allah and being honest, kind, compassionate, generous, loving, forgiving, helpful, and just. Each of us has areas in which we can improve. We need to introspect and figure out exactly what needs improvement, and then should work on improving our character gradually. Each improvement enhances our relationship with Allah and the people in our lives, which in turn leads to improvement in our own levels of fulfilment.

When our jealousy is replaced with genuine happiness for the success of others, then we can relax and simply be happy for others instead of plotting their downfall. When our hatred is replaced with love, we find more reasons to be happy with our lives. When arrogance is replaced with humility, we find peace and joy in the little things in life. Happiness is internal, so finding it means fixing the internal. Replacing bad character with good character is an important part of that process.

KEEP THE DETAILS OF YOUR LIFE PRIVATE

The Messenger ﷺ said, "Seek help in the fulfilment of your needs by being discreet, for everyone who is given a blessing will be envied."

(Al-Mu'jam al-Kabir 16644)

We live in an age of overexposure. Social media has become a playground for showing off the most private details of one's life. The short hits of dopamine we receive from people liking our content delude us into thinking that we are experiencing happiness, but we often do not see the long-term negative effects of such overexposure.

The level of detail that people share about their lives these days is unnatural and very new. The long-term results of this new practice may only be discovered decades from now, when it will be too late for many people. Even in its infancy, we already see many harms arising from this practice. Oversharing has led to unhappiness with one's accomplishments and relationships, excessive jealousy, and the breakdown of many relationships.

While oversharing is new and unnatural, the Islamic way is far closer to human nature. Islam values privacy and teaches us to keep the details of our personal lives a secret. Share your happiness and successes with those closest to you, those who will be happy for you, but the whole world does not need to know about the details of your life. This may lead to malice, jealousy, the evil eye, and even attempts at sabotage.

When you live a private life, you will experience deeper levels of happiness. You will not need to worry about your haters or jealous people, because your focus is on what matters. Try it, and you will be surprised to learn that there is more joy in enjoying a cup of coffee in private than in sharing a picture of it on social media for your friends to see.

The secret to a happy life is to know the limits of what should and should not be shared in public.

Take a step back and re-evaluate your usage of social media. Limit your time on these apps and use them only to post beneficial content that brings people closer to Allah. Spend more time in the real world. Spend time with your family with your social media turned off and the phone silenced.

Be intentional in your privacy. The less society knows about your private life, the happier your life will be. You will experience higher levels of contentment, inner peace, and blessings when you avoid the public eye.

MIND YOUR OWN BUSINESS

The Messenger ﷺ said, "Part of the perfection of one's Islam is his leaving that which does not concern him."

(Tirmidhi 2318)

A lot of problems begin when we poke our nose where it does not belong. Being over-inquisitive about the private details of other people's lives is the beginning of drama and personal problems. This is a violation of people's privacy and a gateway to various sins like gossip, slander, backbiting, breaking ties, and jealousy. All of this can be avoided by following one simple Islamic principle: mind your own business.

The early Muslims mastered this art of minding their own business. There are many great examples of this. One such example is Sa'id ibn Zayd ﷺ, one of the blessed ten who were given the glad tidings of Paradise by the Prophet ﷺ. However, out of the ten of them, he is the one we know the least about.

Despite being one of the first Muslims and having lived a long life, we barely know anything about Sa'id bn Zayd ﷺ. We know that he was the brother-in-law of Umar ibn al-Khattab ﷺ, and it was at his home that Umar ﷺ first read a passage from the Qur'an and recognized the truth of Islam. We know that he fought alongside the Prophet ﷺ in the major battles during his lifetime, and we know that he eventually retired to a small estate outside Madinah.

The details of the twenty years he spent in this estate are unknown. For the most part, he minded his own business, and others did the same too. Sa'id ﷺ led a quiet life focused on worshipping Allah and caring for his family. He avoided drama and personal strife and remained focused on his own spiritual journey for the bulk of his life. We may not know all the details, but we do know that overall Sa'id lived a long, peaceful, happy life. A primary contributing factor to this was his dedication to minding his own business. He was not the only companion to live like this. There are many other great examples like this in our history.

A primary aspect of minding one's own business is to not concern oneself with the private sins of others. Every human is flawed and has their private sins. These mistakes are kept secret by Allah; it is not our job to seek them out or expose them. This does not mean that we should avoid commanding the good and forbidding evil. If evil is done openly, we must condemn it, but we should do so in generic terms without singling people out.

However, if someone's sins are private, then it is not our business. If we stumble upon their secrets, we should keep it secret and advise them in private. It is a sin to expose the sins of others or gossip about them. Just as we want Allah to keep our secret sins hidden, we must do the same for others. The Prophet ﷺ said, "Whoever conceals the sin of a Muslin in this world Allah will conceal his sins on the Last Day." (Sahih Muslim 2590)

Focus on your own spiritual journey and call other to Islam without picking on their personal flaws or seeking out their private matters. This one principle of minding one's own business plays a major role in helping one live a happy, peaceful life.

يَا أَيُّهَا الَّذِينَ آمَنُوا اجْتَنِبُوا كَثِيرًا مِنَ الظَّنِّ إِنَّ بَعْضَ الظَّنِّ إِثْمٌ وَلَا تَجَسَّسُوا وَلَا يَغْتَب بَعْضُكُم بَعْضًا أَيُحِبُّ أَحَدُكُمْ أَنْ يَأْكُلَ لَحْمَ أَخِيهِ مَيْتًا فَكَرِهْتُمُوهُ وَاتَّقُوا اللَّهَ إِنَّ اللَّهَ تَوَّابٌ رَحِيمٌ

Yaaa ayyuhal lazeena aamanuj taniboo kaseeram minaz zanni inna ba'daz zanniismunw wa laa tajassasoo wa la yaghtab ba'dukum ba'daa; a yuhibbu ahadukum any yaakula lahma akheehi maitan fakarih tumooh; wattaqul laa; innal laaha tawwaabur Raheem

O you who believe, avoid suspicion because most suspicion is sinful, and do not spy on each other, and do not backbite each other. Would you like to eat the flesh of your dead brother? No, you would hate it. So be conscious of Allah. Indeed, Allah is Forgiving, Merciful (Surah al-Hujarat 49:12)

BE HONEST AND SPEAK THE TRUTH

The Messenger ﷺ said, "You must be truthful. Verily, truthfulness leads to righteousness and righteousness leads to Paradise. A man continues to be truthful and encourages honesty until he is recorded with Allah as truthful."

(Sahih al-Bukhari 6094 & Sahih Muslim 2607)

Honesty is the hallmark of a Muslim's personality. The Prophet ﷺ was known for his honesty, even before Islam. Because he was such an honest person, his companions like Abu Bakr ؓ, Uthman ؓ, and Khadija ؓ believed in him immediately. Even the Caesar of Rome stated that if he did not lie about worldly things, why would he lie about God, which is the most severe thing to lie about. His honesty was a crucial part of his Dawah. Many early converts accepted Islam immediately because they knew him as an honest man.

When Muslims are honest, it reflects well on Islam. Our character becomes a means of attracting people to the religion. Islam spread to the Indonesian and

Malaysian islands through interactions with honest Muslim traders. People were amazed by the level of character and integrity that Islam inspired in its followers, and this attracted them to Islam.

Honest people have nothing to hide. They do not need to worry about getting exposed or caught out, and they do not need to build more lies to cover their previous lies. They are at peace. Knowing that they are honest in their business, family, and social life, they have nothing to hide, and this allows them to sleep in peace every night.

Honesty in business means being transparent about your goods and services. A business run on lies is eventually bound to be exposed and can only lead to humiliation. An honest trader does not hide defects, falsely advertise, or deceive customers. People want to trade with him because they respect his honesty and love him for his integrity.

Honesty in family life means having good relationships with your family built on trust and open communication. An honest man does not have secret lovers or secret families; the trust between husband and wife is very difficult to rebuild once it has been broken. Honesty in family is about transparency and trust.

Honesty in social dealings means being a person others can turn to for clear advice. True believers advise gently yet honestly because they want what is best for their fellow Muslims. People value their honesty because they know they are getting the real deal and not fake friendship. Honest people are not two-faced, do not carry tales, and avoid gossip. They are an asset to every friend and colleague and are people they can trust with their lives and wealth.

Honest people live in peace. They lack enemies because they have nothing to hide, and people love and respect them. Their families are loyal to them, and so are their customers and friends. Honesty really is the best policy.

REFLECT ON PARADISE

The Messenger ﷺ said, "The most miserable people in the world among the people of Paradise will come on the Day of Resurrection to be dipped in Paradise, then it will be said: 'O son of Adam, did you see any hardship? Did you have any distress?' He will say: 'No, by Allah, my Lord! I did not once see hardship or distress.'"

(Sahih Muslim 2807)

Life can be hard, and we cannot be happy all the time. Our lives will go through ups and downs at different points. We will all face difficulties and tragedies at some point. This is an inevitable part of the human experience. When the pain gets too much, the only way to move on is to remember that this world is temporary and eternal bliss lies on the other side.

Paradise is an eternal home of bliss for the believer. It is a special reward that Allah has created for those who choose to live in a way that is pleasing to Him. He has created in Paradise that which no eye has seen, no ear has heard, and no mind has even imagined. The delights and pleasures of Paradise are beyond human imagination.

So great are the pleasures of Paradise that a person who suffered throughout their worldly life may enter Paradise for a moment and forget all his worldly pain. The eternal garden is the true happiness that every believer seeks. It is here where we will live forever in a state of eternal bliss, pleased and pleasing to Allah.

Humans make the mistake of thinking they can achieve true happiness in this world. But our happiness in this world comes and goes. We will have sad days and happy days, days of celebration and days of sorrow. We will face trials but also enjoy blessings. Life is temporary, all of it, the good and the bad. Even happiness in this world is temporary.

If we truly desire a life of happiness, our focus needs to be beyond this world. Real happiness is in Paradise. When we live our lives focused on pleasing Allah, He will make the tough times manageable, and bless our hearts with contentment, inner peace, and happiness, whenever we need it. He will guide our actions and open the doors of victory for us. If we pass away as believers, having tried our best to obey Allah, then He may enter us into His Paradise, out of His Mercy.

None of us can say that we are perfect or pious enough to be worthy of Paradise. It is a blessing that Allah grants through His Compassion and Mercy to those who sincerely try to obey Him. So, we spend our lives trying our best. Every time we slip up, we repent and try again. Our goal is simple: to strive to live a life that is pleasing to the Creator and, in the process, earn His Pleasure and enter Paradise in a state of eternal bliss.

يَا أَيَّتُهَا النَّفْسُ الْمُطْمَئِنَّةُ
ارْجِعِي إِلَى رَبِّكِ رَاضِيَةً مَرْضِيَّةً
فَادْخُلِي فِي عِبَادِي
وَادْخُلِي جَنَّتِي

Yaaa ayyatuhan nafsul mutma 'innah
Irji'eee ilaa Rabbiki raadiyatam mardiyyah
Fadkhulee fee 'ibaadee
Wadkhulee jannatee

O soul that is in a state of peace,
return to your Lord happy and pleasing (to Him).
So, enter among My worshippers,
you will enter My Paradise

(Surah al-Fajr 89:27–30)

THE KEYS ARE IN
YOUR HANDS

These 25 keys can open the doors of true happiness for the believer. Happiness does not lie in fleeting moments of sensual pleasure or in chasing wealth and fame. Happiness is a gift from Allah to those who choose to live a life that is pleasing to Him.

To find real happiness, we must understand our relationship with Allah. Allah created us to worship their. Happiness, therefore, lies in living a life that is pleasing to Him. By focusing on Allah, building our afterlife, and reframing our minds to think positively about Allah, we can unlock the inner secrets of true happiness.

Happiness in our personal lives lies in forming beautiful relationships that are pleasing to Allah. This begins with our relationship with our parents. By nurturing that relationship, as well as our relationships with our spouses, children, friends, and communities, we can build beautiful ties that produce powerful memories together.

How we conduct ourselves and deal with others plays an important role in maintaining our own inner peace. Developing a strong work ethic, being optimistic, honest, and selfless, and trying our best to always display the best of manners and character. These are all keys to true happiness.

Finally, it is important to make peace with the fact that life in this world will end, and real happiness can only be experienced in the next world. To remember death, to strive for Paradise, and to endure the trials of this world patiently are all keys to unlocking eternal happiness in the next life.

The keys are now in your hands. It is up to you to use them properly. These simple principles demonstrate the beauty and eternal wisdom of Islam. They are crucial for living to our full potential and becoming models of faith, piety, and inner peace. Remember that real pleasure lies in the pleasure of Allah, so strive for His Pleasure always.

ISMAIL KAMDAR

ABOUT THE AUTHOR

Shaykh Ismail Kamdar is a graduate of a traditional Alim program (Talimudin, 2006). He also holds a Bachelor's in Islamic Studies (International Open University, 2014). He has studied Islam in both traditional and modern settings and has been a student of Islamic Studies for almost two decades.

He began studying Islam full-time at the age of thirteen, began preaching at the age of sixteen, and wrote his first book at the age of twenty-three. Over the years, he has taught multiple courses and seminars around the world and has worked with multiple leading Islamic organizations across the globe.

Shaykh Ismail Kamdar currently works as a researcher at Yaqeen Institute for Islamic Research. He is also the founder of Islamic Self Help and Izzah Academy. Shaykh Ismail specializes in Fiqh, Tafsir, and History, and is the author of over twenty books in the fields of Islamic Studies and personal development.

OTHER BOOKS BY ISMAIL KAMDAR

Getting the Barakah: An Islamic Guide to Time Management

Best of Creation: An Islamic Guide to Self-Confidence

Earning Barakah: An Islamic Guide to Blessed Sustenance

Qur'an 30for30: The Companion Reader

Qur'an 30for30: Seerah Edition

Qur'an 30for30: Judgment Day Edition

The Shukr Lifestyle: A Gratitude Journal

Ahmad Climbs a Mountain: A Parable about Achieving Your Goal

Homeschooling 101: What to Expect in Your First Year

Having Fun the Halal Way: Entertainment in Islam

Productivity Principles Of 'Umar II: 'Umar bin 'Abd al-'Aziz

Themes of the Qur'an

The Greeting of Peace

The Book of Hope for Sinners

10 Self-Help Tips from 10 Authentic Hadiths

Discover Your Hidden Gems

Discover Your Confidence

Information about each of these books can be found at
books.islamicselfhelp.com

Websites:

Islamic Self Help
http://islamicselfhelp.com

Izzah Academy
http://izzahacademy.com

Social Media:

Facebook Page
https://www.facebook.com/ShIsmailKamdar

Twitter Handle
https://twitter.com/IsmailKamdar

YouTube Channel
https://www.youtube.com/c/IsmailKamdar

Audio Lecture Stream
https://www.muslimcentralaudio.com/category/ismail-kamdar/